Math on the Playground
Area and Perimeter

Ian F. Mahaney

PowerKiDS press™
New York

Published in 2013 by The Rosen Publishing Group, Inc.
29 East 21st Street, New York, NY 10010

First Edition

Editor: Joanne Randolph
Book Design: Greg Tucker

Photo Credits: Cover Digital Vision/Photodisc/Getty Images; pp. 4–5 Gregory Johnston/Shutterstock.com; pp. 6, 12–13 iStockphoto/Thinkstock; p. 7 Tracy Whiteside/Shutterstock.com; p. 9 (top) Henryk Sadura/Shutterstock.com; pp. 10–11 Jack Schiffer/Shutterstock.com; pp. 14–15 JoeJayphotos/Shutterstock.com; p. 16 Stockbyte/Thinkstock; p. 17 © Jim West/age fotostock; p. 18 ERproductions Ltd./Blend Images/Getty Images; p. 19 Tobik/Shutterstock.com; pp. 20–21 Kiselev Andrey Valerevich/Shutterstock.com.

Library of Congress Cataloging-in-Publication Data

Mahaney, Ian F.
  Math on the playground : area and perimeter / by Ian F. Mahaney. — 1st ed.
      p. cm. — (Core math skills)
  Includes index.
  ISBN 978-1-4488-9657-8 (library binding) — ISBN 978-1-4488-9772-8 (pbk.) —
  ISBN 978-1-4488-9773-5 (6-pack)
  1. Area measurement—Juvenile literature. 2. Perimeters (Geometry)—Juvenile literature. 3. Playgrounds—Juvenile literature. I. Title.
  QC104.5.M34 2013
  516'.154—dc23
                                    2012026333

Manufactured in the United States of America

CPSIA Compliance Information: Batch #W13PK4: For Further Information contact Rosen Publishing, New York, New York at 1-800-237-9932

Contents

Math at the Playground

There's a lot of math at a playground. You can figure out what **fraction** of kids can use the swings at once. You can also measure the border of the playground.

Knowing the **dimensions** of the playground can help you understand **perimeter** and **area**. The perimeter is the **boundary** of the playground. You measure it by adding the lengths of each side of the playground. Area is the amount of space the playground takes up. Knowing the area of a playground helps you understand the size of the playground.

Area and perimeter will also help you compare playgrounds. A playground with a 220-foot perimeter has a larger perimeter than a playground with a perimeter of 210 feet: 220 > 210.

Conversion Box
1 foot = .3 meter

You could measure the perimeter of each triangle on this dome at the playground.

Which playground has a larger perimeter?

Name	Perimeter
Raleigh Street Playground	332 feet
17th Avenue Playground	323 feet

(See answers on p. 22)

Figure It Out

How Big Around?

Playgrounds come in all shapes and sizes. A lot of playgrounds are rectangles. You can measure each side of the rectangle. The sum of the length of the sides is the perimeter. If the sides of a rectangular playground measure 30 feet and 50 feet, the perimeter is 30 feet + 30 feet + 50 feet + 50 feet = 160 feet. Another way to **express** this is (2 x 30 feet) + (2 x 50 feet) = 60 feet + 100 feet = 160 feet.

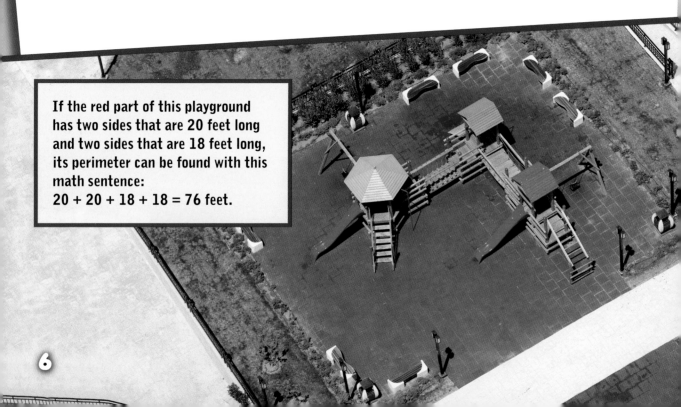

If the red part of this playground has two sides that are 20 feet long and two sides that are 18 feet long, its perimeter can be found with this math sentence:
20 + 20 + 18 + 18 = 76 feet.

There are many ways to measure perimeter. You can measure it with a yardstick, measuring tape, or your feet.

A ruler or yardstick is a tool for measuring. While you could use a yardstick or a ruler to measure a playground, it might take a while to do it this way. It could be a good way to practice your addition or multiplication, though!

Conversion Box
1 foot = .3 meter
1 square foot = .09 square meter

What is the perimeter of a square playground where one of the sides is 40 feet long?

(See answers on p. 22)

Figure It Out

Tile It!

A unit square is a square 1 unit long and 1 unit wide. The unit of measure could be feet, meters, or some other measure. A water fountain is a unit square that is about 1 foot long and 1 foot wide. It is measured as 1 foot x 1 foot = 1 square foot.

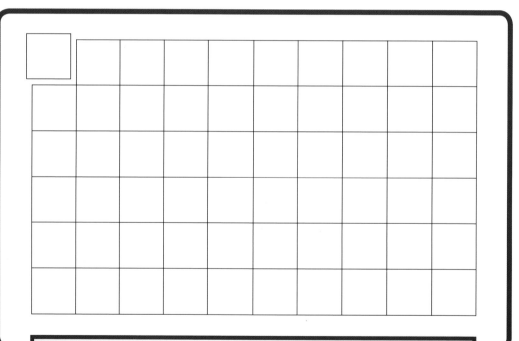

In this diagram, a water fountain would fit 60 times in this small playground. Since 60 water fountains would fit inside the playground, the playground is 60 x 1 square foot = 60 square feet.

A water fountain can be used to measure the area of a playground. To find the area, figure out how many water fountains would fit in a playground, as shown in the **diagram** on page 8. This way of **calculating** is called **tiling**.

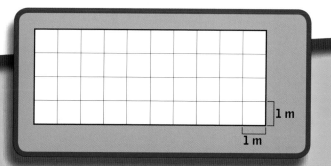

1 m

1 m

Figure It Out

This rectangular playground is covered in rubber squares that are 1 meter long and 1 meter wide. How many square meters is its area?

(See answers on p. 22)

The Area of the Playground

There are other ways to find the area of an object or space. If you know the length and width of a playground, you can find the area. The area is the length of a rectangle times the its width.

Let's say we have a playground that is 20 feet long and 14 feet wide. The area is 20 feet x 14 feet = 280 square feet. That's 280 square feet where you can play and have fun!

Conversion Box
1 foot = .3 meter
1 square foot = .09 square meter

In a playground, the jungle gym, including the slide and monkey bars, is 15 feet long by 6 feet wide. Its area is 15 feet x 6 feet = 90 square feet.

A play structure is 12 feet long and 8 feet wide. What is its area?

(See answers on p. 22)

Figure It Out

If a sandbox is shaped like an L, you can still calculate its area. To calculate this sandbox's area, the sandbox is split into parts. Next, the area of each piece is found, and the areas are added together.

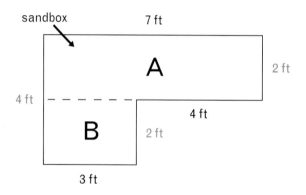

This sandbox has been split into two parts. The area of part A is 7 feet x 2 feet = 14 square feet. The area of part B is 3 feet x 2 feet = 6 square feet. The area of the sandbox is the sum of parts A and B,
14 square feet + 6 square feet = 20 square feet. You can add area!

Conversion Box
1 foot = .3 meter
1 square foot = .09 square meter

There are two sandboxes next to each other. One measures 5 feet by 7 feet. The second measures 7 feet by 5 feet. What is the sandboxes' combined area?

(See answers on p. 22)

Figure It Out

Lawn Versus Wood Chips

There are often two parts of a playground. There is a lawn on the outside for running around and wood chips inside where the swings and slides are. If you know the area of the playground and the area of the wood chips, you can subtract to find the area of the lawn.

In this diagram, the area of the playground is 42 feet x 32 feet = 1,344 square feet. The area of the wood chips is 22 feet x 26 feet = 572 square feet. The grass is the difference:

1,344 square feet – 572 square feet = 772 square feet.

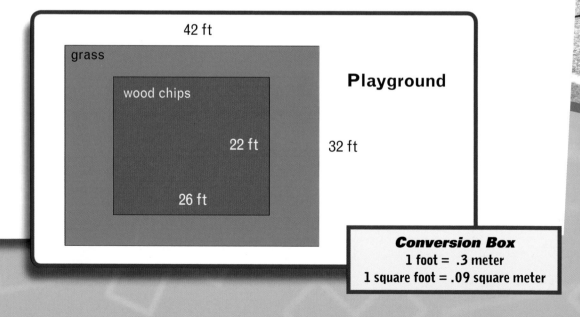

42 ft

grass

wood chips

Playground

22 ft

32 ft

26 ft

Conversion Box
1 foot = .3 meter
1 square foot = .09 square meter

A playground is 23 feet long and 20 feet wide. The wood chips inside are a square, and each side is 12 feet long. What is the area of the lawn?

(See answers on p. 22)

Cleanup Crew

Nine volunteers offer to clean up a playground that has a perimeter of 180 feet and an area of 2,000 square feet. One volunteer will walk the perimeter and collect trash. The other eight volunteers will split up the area.

Graph paper is a good tool to use when trying to find the area of things. If you know your object has a length of 10 units and width of 5, you can count out the boxes on the paper.

To figure out how much area each volunteer needs to clean, divide the area by the number of volunteers: 2,000 square feet ÷ 8 = 250 square feet each.

You can multiply and divide area, too. If five volunteers each clean up 30 square feet of a playground, they clean up 30 square feet x 5 = 150 square feet together.

Conversion Box
1 foot = .3 meter
1 square foot = .09 square meter

If eight volunteers clean up a playground that is 60 feet long by 40 feet wide, how much area does each one have to clean?

(See answers on p. 22)

Figure It Out

Monkeying Around

For monkey bars that are 10 feet long and 3 feet wide, their perimeter is 10 feet + 3 feet + 10 feet + 3 feet = 26 feet. If there are 10 bars along the length of the monkey bars, making 10 squares, you can figure out the area of each square.

String can be used to measure larger objects, such as the length and width of the monkey bars. Afterward, measure the rope to calculate the perimeter or the area.

To find the area, we first need to find out the length of each square. Divide the total length of the side by the number of squares: 10 ÷ 10 = 1. Then multiply the length times the width of 3 feet: 1 x 3 = 3 square feet. Now you can multiply the area of one square by 10 and get the area for the entire set of monkey bars: 10 x 3 = 30. Get swinging!

Conversion Box
1 foot = .3 meter
1 square foot = .09 square meter

What is the perimeter of monkey bars that are 9 feet long and 3 feet wide? What is their area?

(See answers on p. 22)

Figure It Out

Math Fun at the Playground

You have learned a few **methods** for calculating perimeter and area. There are other ways to calculate area on a playground, though. One is by using the **distributive property** of multiplication. The distributive property of multiplication says that you can break up larger numbers, multiply the smaller numbers, and then add the results together.

If a playground is 43 feet long by 40 feet wide, you can find the area this way:

43 feet x 40 feet = (40 feet + 3 feet) x 40 feet =

(40 feet x 40 feet) + (3 feet x 40 feet) =

1,600 square feet + 120 square feet =

1,720 square feet. There are lots of ways to learn about area and perimeter on the playground!

Conversion Box
1 foot = .3 meter
1 square foot = .09 square meter

What other kinds of math can you do at the playground? You can count the swings, measure the slide, and so much more. Have some fun with math next time you are at the playground!

What is the area of a playground that is 64 feet long and 30 feet wide?

(See answers on p. 22)

Figure It Out

Figure It Out: The Answers

Page 5: **The Raleigh Street Playground has a larger perimeter: 332 feet > 323 feet.**

Page 7: **The perimeter of this playground is 40 feet + 40 feet + 40 feet + 40 feet = 160 feet. Another way to express this is 4 x 40 feet = 160 feet.**

Page 9: **The playground's area is 40 x 1 square meter = 40 square meters. This means that 40 rubber squares fit in this playground.**

Page 11: **The area is 12 feet x 8 feet = 96 square feet.**

Page 13: **The first sandbox's area is 5 feet x 7 feet = 35 square feet. The second sandbox's area is 7 feet x 5 feet = 35 square feet. Combined, the area of the sandboxes is 35 square feet + 35 square feet = 70 square feet.**

Page 15: **The area of the playground is 23 feet x 20 feet = 460 square feet. The area of the wood chips is 12 feet x 12 feet = 144 square feet. The area of the lawn is the difference, 460 square feet – 144 square feet = 316 square feet.**

Page 17: **The area of the playground is 60 feet x 40 feet = 2,400 square feet. Each volunteer will clean 2,400 square feet ÷ 8 = 300 square feet.**

Page 19: **The monkey bars are 9 feet + 9 feet + 3 feet + 3 feet = 24 feet around and 9 feet x 3 feet = 27 square feet in area.**

Page 21: **Using the distributive property of multiplication, 64 feet x 30 feet = (60 feet + 4 feet) x 30 feet = (60 feet x 30 feet) + (4 feet x 30 feet) = 1,800 square feet + 120 square feet = 1,920 square feet.**

Conversion Box
1 foot = .3 meter
1 square foot = .09 square meter

Glossary

area (ER-ee-uh) A measure of a space.

boundary (BOWN-duh-ree) The border that separates one area from another.

calculating (KAL-kyuh-layt-ing) Figuring out with math.

diagram (DY-uh-gram) A picture of something.

dimensions (duh-MEN-shunz) The length, width, or height of an object.

distributive property (dih-STRIH-byoo-tiv PRO-pur-tee) A rule in multiplication that allows bigger numbers to be split into smaller numbers.

express (ik-SPRES) To say mathematically.

fraction (FRAK-shun) A part of something that is bigger.

methods (MEH-thudz) Ways of doing things.

perimeter (peh-RIH-meh-tur) The outline of a place or thing.

tiling (TY-ul-ing) Measuring an object by filling it with square units.

Index

Websites

Due to the changing nature of Internet links, PowerKids Press has developed an online list of websites related to the subject of this book. This site is updated regularly. Please use this link to access the list: www.powerkidslinks.com/cms/play/